Double Wedding Ring

The Classic QUILT Series #1

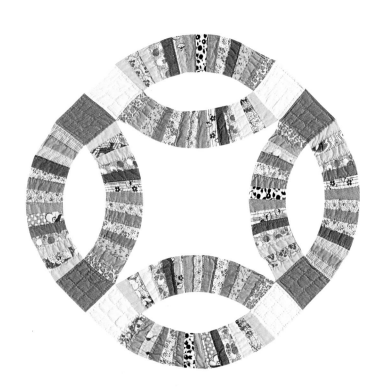

LAURA NOWNES

The Quilt Digest Press

Editorial and production direction by Michael Kile.
Book editing by Harold Nadel.
Book and cover design by Kajun Graphics.
Quilt photography by Sharon Risedorph and Karen
Steffens.
Cover and room setting photographs by Sharon
Risedorph.
Computer graphics by Kandy Petersen.
Typographical composition by DC Typography.
Printed by Nissha Printing Company, Ltd., Kyoto, Japan.
Color separations by the printer.
Home graciously lent by Michael and Marion Gates.

For my Dad, with love.

Second Printing.

Library of Congress Cataloging-in-Publication Data

Nownes, Laura, 1953-
    Double wedding ring / Laura Nownes.
        p.   cm.
    ISBN 0-913327-23-9 (pbk.) : $6.95
    1. Quilting–Patterns. 2. Double wedding ring quilts. I. Title.
    TT835.N68   1990
    745.9'7–dc20
                                                    90-42335
                                                       CIP

The Quilt Digest Press
P.O. Box 1331
Gualala, CA 95445

INTRODUCTION

There's no pattern as popular as *Double Wedding Ring;* since its appearance in the early twentieth century, more *Double Wedding Ring*s have been made than any other pattern. When I first saw a *Double Wedding Ring* quilt, at the Mormon Handicraft Shop in Utah, I fell in love with it and decided to make one for myself. As a novice quiltmaker, though, I was very frustrated by it: I was not able to make the pieces fit together and lie flat, despite being an experienced and meticulous seamstress.

Since my initial experience with this pattern many years ago, new and better methods of construction have been introduced. The method I have devised and which I present here is another option which I feel comfortable with and which works well for me. I am confident that, if *you* take the time, you too will make beautiful *Double Wedding Ring* quilts easily.

Here are three absolutely glorious *Double Wedding Ring* quilt variations—and, as a special bonus, a table runner—for your sewing enjoyment. Each quilt is different from the others, giving you a chance to choose which *Double Wedding Ring* variation you

want to make *first.* And the table runner is a quick, easy project to dress up your dining table—or to give as a gift to a special friend.

For each quilt and the runner you will find:
- A full-color photograph
- A size chart
- A yardage chart
- Cutting instructions
- Sewing instructions
- Accurate templates

The templates and construction methods used here are brand new, created just for this book. I've tested them and they make perfect *Double Wedding Ring* projects each and every time. Follow the instructions carefully and each *Double Wedding Ring* you create will indeed be an heirloom to treasure.

Happy quilting!

Laura

Laura Nownes

WHAT YOU NEED

Fabric: 100% cotton: see individual quilts for exact amounts. 8″ × 8″ piece of muslin for single arc guide
Template plastic
Ultra-fine permanent pen
Paper scissors
Marking pencil
Glass-head pins
Fabric scissors
Sewing machine or hand sewing needle
100% cotton thread
Steam iron
Light-colored towel
Pressing surface
Batting

MAKING YOUR RINGS

A ¼″ seam is used throughout. Carefully read all of these instructions before you begin, as well as the specifics for the individual quilt.

Make a plastic template for each of the shapes required for the quilt you are making. Transfer the dots and centerpoint markings indicated on the center and melon shapes to the plastic templates. You will notice that only one quarter of the center shape is shown. I recommend that you make a complete center shape from template plastic: you will achieve a more accurate fabric shape than if you made only one quarter and placed it on the fold of the fabric.

Use the plastic shapes to trace the required number of pieces onto the fabric. Cut the shapes apart with your fabric scissors. Transfer the dots and centerpoint markings onto the wrong side of each center and melon fabric piece.

You will notice that many of the rings in these quilts appear distorted or squashed. This is partly a result of inconsistency in the melon shapes. Chances are that the pieced arcs varied in size, so adjustments were made to the melon shapes. We have done our best to present you with an accurate rendition of the patterns as shown, with corrections for inconsistencies in individual shapes.

The manner of construction presented here is just one of the many possibilities available for this pattern. I believe, however, that one of the secrets to the success of this pattern is the accuracy of the pieced arcs. The more segments contained within the pieced arc, the greater the chance for unintentional variation in size! A template pattern for a single arc is given for each quilt. It gives you the option of making each quilt with a single arc variation; even more importantly, it is required for testing the accuracy of your pieced arcs. For those quilts which have pieced arcs, I urge you to make a single arc of your quilt from a piece of muslin. Next, make one pieced arc unit, referring to Steps 1 through 3 below for help. Compare the size and shape of your pieced arc with the muslin guide. The two must be the same to avoid construction problems. This test will allow you to see if your fabric pieces were cut accurately or if adjustments are needed in the width of your seam. The extra time spent at this point will pay off in the end. You will finish with neat, flat rings. Only after you feel confident with the size and shape of your pieced arc, proceed as follows:

1. For quilts with pieced arcs, join the required number of fabric segment pieces together, as shown in the illustration. For the quilt with solid arcs, proceed to Step 4.

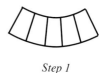

Step 1

2. Attach two end pieces to the joined segments to complete the pieced arc, as shown in the illustration. Note: all quilts with the exception of the Traditional have end pieces.
3. Press all of the seams to one direction.

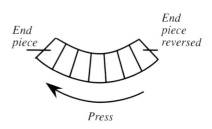

Steps 2-3

4. With their right sides together and center points matching, place a center shape on top of an arc section. The dots on the center shape should come to within ¼″ of the end of the arc section. Pin at the center and ends, then secure at intermediate points. Note that the arc and the center shape, when placed right sides together, must curve in opposite directions in

order for the sewn edge to match the illustration.

5. Join the arc to the center shape, stitching from end to end.

6. Sew another arc to the opposite side of the center shape, as shown in the illustration.

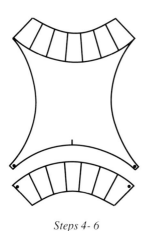

Steps 4- 6

7. Press the seams in the direction of the arc sections.

8. Sew arc sections to the other sides of each center shape, as shown in the illustration.

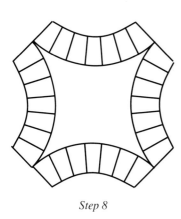

Step 8

9. Press the seams in the direction of the arc sections.

10. Join posts together in pairs to make post units, as indicated by the individual quilt and as shown in the illustration.

Color One   *Color Two*

Step 10

11. Join the post units to the corners of the required number of center/arc units (as indicated in each quilt) to make Unit A, as shown in the illustration.

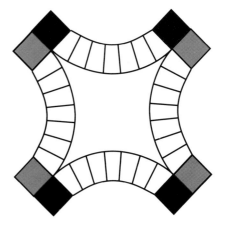

Unit A
Step 11

12. With the melon shape on top and their center-points matching, right sides together, attach melon shapes to the required number of center/arc units (as indicated in each quilt) to make Unit B, as shown in the illustration. Be careful, as the seams of the segments will be facing away from you and could inadvertently be pushed by the feed dog.

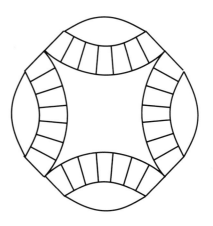

Unit B
Step 12

13. Make the required number of arc/post units (Unit C), as indicated in each quilt and as shown in the illustration.

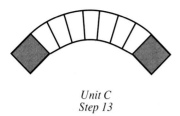

Unit C
Step 13

14. Make the required number of arc/melon units (Unit D), as indicated in each quilt and as shown in the illustration.

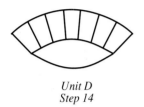

Unit D
Step 14

15. Lay out all of the units onto a flat surface, similar to the layout in the illustration.

16. Join the A and B Units, starting and stopping ¼″ from each end of the arcs on the A Units, as indicated by the dots in the illustration.

17. Attach Units C and D around the outer edges, starting and stopping ¼″ from each end of the arcs on Unit C, as indicated by the dots in the illustration.

18. Join the posts around the outer edge, as indicated by the arrows in the illustration. Stitch only up to the dot.

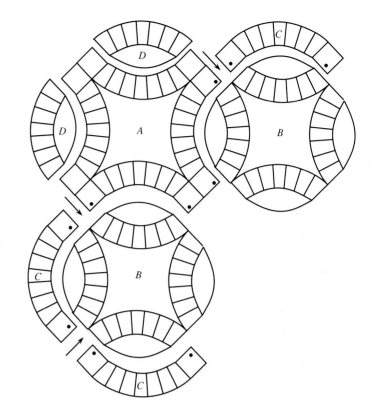

Made by Marguerite Philips, Carlsbad, New Mexico, c.1940. Collection of Janet Carruth.

21½″ Ring

	CRIB/WALL	TWIN	DOUBLE/QUEEN	KING
Finished size	49″×63″	77″×91″	91″×91″	105″×105″
Rings set	3×4	5×6	6×6	7×7

FABRIC NEEDED (YARDS)

Background fabric (includes one post)	1½	3¼	3¾	5
Pieced arcs	2½	5½	6¼	8¼
Posts: Color Two	⅜	⅝	¾	⅞
Backing	4	5½	8	9½
Binding (bias)	¾	1	1¼	1¼

CUTTING YOUR FABRIC

Use Templates A, B, C, D and E (single arc guide).

Background fabric:				
Center: Template A	12	30	36	49
Melon: Template D	31	71	84	112
Post: Template C	32	72	84	112
Pieced arcs: Template B	868	1988	2352	3136
Post, Color Two: Template C	36	80	94	124
Backing: number of lengths	2	2	3	3

PUTTING IT ALL TOGETHER

# of Unit A	6	15	18	25
# of Unit B	6	15	18	24
# of Unit C	7	11	12	12
# of Unit D	7	11	12	16
# of post units	24	60	72	100

1. Make a sample pieced arc using template B pieces, as shown in the illustration. Note that there are no end pieces for this pattern. Test its size against a single arc template E piece for accuracy. Make any necessary adjustments.

2. Make the remaining pieced arcs.

3. Join all of the pieced arcs to all of the center shapes, as shown in the illustration.

4. Join a post of color one to a post of color two to make the required number of post units, as shown in the illustration.

5. Join the post units to the required number of center/arc units to form Unit A. Note the exact placement of the posts, as shown in the illustration.

6. Add melons to the remaining center/arc units to make Unit B, as shown in the illustration.

7. Make the required number of Unit C's, making one-half with color one posts and one-half with color two posts, as shown in the illustrations.

8. Add melons to the remaining pieced arcs to make the Unit D's.

Step 1

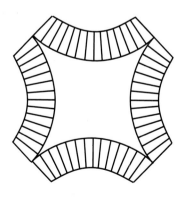

Step 3

9. Join all of the units together, referring to the assembly illustration in the general instructions.

10. Your quilt top is now ready to be layered and quilted.

11. Finish the edges with a narrow bias binding.

Step 4

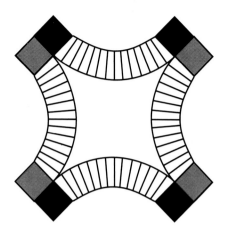

Unit A
Step 5

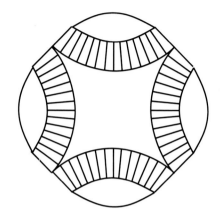

Unit B
Step 6

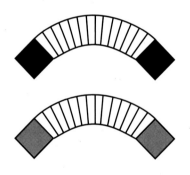

Unit C
Step 7

Unit D
Step 8

Step 9

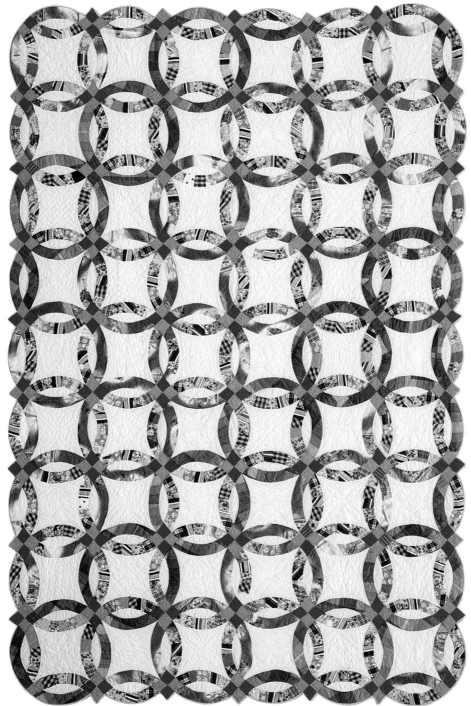

Maker unknown, c.1950. Collection of Robert and Ardis James.

13½″ Ring

	CRIB/WALL	TWIN	DOUBLE/QUEEN	KING
Finished size	42″ × 60″	70″ × 89″	89″ × 89″	98″ × 98″
Rings set	4 × 6	7 × 9	9 × 9	10 × 10

FABRIC NEEDED (YARDS)

Background fabric	1½	4	5	6
Prints for arcs	2	4½	5½	6½
Posts: Color One	⅜	½	⅝	¾
Color Two	⅜	½	⅝	¾
Backing	1⅞	5½	8	8
Binding (bias)	¾	1	1¼	1¼

CUTTING YOUR FABRIC

Use templates M, N, O, P, Q and R.

Background fabric:				
Center: Template M	24	63	81	100
Melon: Template Q	58	142	180	220
Single arcs: Template R	58	142	180	220
Pieced arcs:				
Segment: Template N	174	438	552	660
End piece: Template O	58 &	142 &	180 &	220 &
	58R	142R	180R	220R
Posts: Template P				
Colors One and Two, *each*	68	156	196	238
Backing: number of lengths	1	2	3	3
R = reverse template on fabric				

PUTTING IT ALL TOGETHER

# of Unit A	12	32	41	50
# of Unit B	12	31	40	50
# of Unit C	10	14	16	20
# of Unit D	10	18	20	20
# of post units	48	128	164	200

1. Make a sample pieced arc using template pieces N and O, as shown in the illustration. Then test its size against a single arc template R piece for accuracy. Make any necessary adjustments.

2. Make the remaining pieced arcs.

3. Join the pieced arcs to the required number of center shapes for Unit A's.

4. Join a post of color one to a post of color two to make the required number of post units, as shown in the illustration.

5. To make Unit A: Join the post units to the center/pieced arc units. Note the exact placement of the posts, as shown in the illustration.

6. To make Unit B: Join the single arcs to the required number of center shapes. Then add melons to each unit, as shown in the illustration.

7. Add a post of color one and a post of color two to the remaining pieced arcs to make Unit C, as shown in the illustration.

8. Add a melon to each of the remaining single arcs to form Unit D, as shown in the illustration.

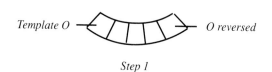

Template O — O reversed

Step 1

Color Two — Color One

Step 4

9. Join all of the units together, referring to the assembly illustration.

10. Add the remaining posts around the edges, as shown in the illustration, stitching only up to the previous stitching lines.

11. Your quilt top is ready to be layered and quilted.

12. Finish the edges with a narrow bias binding.

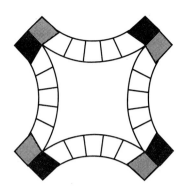

Unit A
Step 5

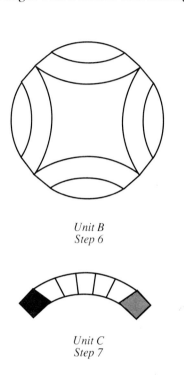

Unit B
Step 6

Unit C
Step 7

Unit D
Step 8

Steps 9-10
Assembly

AMISH

Amish maker unknown, c.1940. Collection of Robert and Ardis James.

20″ Ring

	CRIB/WALL	TWIN	DOUBLE/QUEEN	KING
Finished size	56″ × 56″	71″ × 84″	84″ × 84″	98″ × 98″
Rings set	3 × 3	4 × 5	5 × 5	6 × 6

FABRIC NEEDED (YARDS)

Background fabric	2½	4	4½	6¼
Color One (Pink) (includes bias binding)	1½	2¼	2¾	3¾
Color Two (Green)	1	1¾	2¼	3
Backing	3½	5	7½	8½

CUTTING YOUR FABRIC

Use templates F, G, H, I, J, K (single arc guide) and L (border curve guide).

Background fabric:				
Border: Four strips, *each* 7½″ ×	46″	75″	75″	89″
Corner squares:	four 7½″ squares for all sizes			
Center: Template F	9	20	25	36
Melon: Template J	24	49	60	84
Color One (Pink):				
Segment: Template G	216	441	540	756
End piece: Template H	24 &	49 &	60 &	84 &
	24R	49R	60R	84R
Post: Template I	24	49	60	84
Color Two (Green):				
Segment: Template G	216	441	540	756
End piece: Template H	24 &	49 &	60 &	84 &
	24R	49R	60R	84R
Post: Template I	24	49	60	84
Backing: number of lengths	2	2	3	3
R = reverse template on fabric				

PUTTING IT ALL TOGETHER

# of Unit A	5	10	13	18
# of Unit B	4	10	12	18
# of Unit C	4	9	8	12
# of Unit D	8	9	12	12
# of post units	20	40	52	72

1. Make a sample pieced arc using template pieces G and H, as shown in the illustration. Then, test its size against single arc template K for accuracy. Make any necessary adjustments.

2. Make the remaining pieced arcs, making one-half beginning and ending with color one end pieces and one-half beginning and ending with color two end pieces.

3. Join the pieced arcs to the center shapes, placing similar combinations on opposite sides, as shown in the illustration.

4. Join a post of color one to a post of color two to make the required number of post units, as shown in the illustration.

5. Join the post units to the required number of center/arc units to form Unit A. Note the exact placement of the posts, as shown in the illustration.

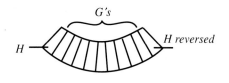

Step 1

6. Add melons to the remaining center/arc units to make Unit B, as shown in the illustration.

7. Make the required number of Unit C's, making one-half with color one posts and one-half with color two posts, as shown in the illustrations.

8. Add melons to the remaining pieced arcs to make the Unit D's, as shown in the illustration.

9. Join all of the units together, referring to the assembly illustration.

10. To make the borders: make a full size plastic model of template L. With the wrong side of the border strip facing up, lay the plastic template on top to mark the curves, repeating as necessary to extend the full length of the border strip, as shown in the illustration. Trim any excess length, remembering to allow ¼″ for seam allowance at each end.

11. Join border strips to two opposite sides of the quilt top, as shown in the illustration.

12. Sew corner squares to the other two border strips. Then join these strips to the quilt top, as shown in the illustration.

13. Your quilt top is now ready to be layered and quilted.

14. Finish the edges with a narrow bias binding.

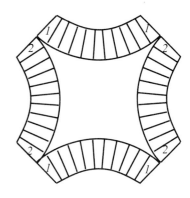

Step 3

Color One   *Color Two*

Step 4

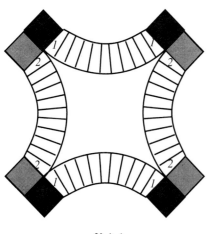

Unit A
Step 5

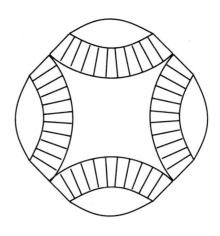

Unit B
Step 6

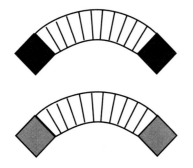

Unit C
Step 7

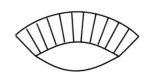

Unit D
Step 8

Step 9

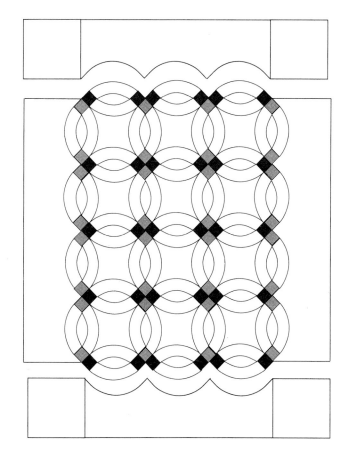

Steps 11-12

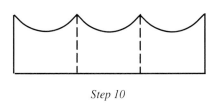

Step 10

TABLE RUNNER

Made by Frances L. Boyle. Courtesy of Stitches 'n Stuffing, Naperville, Illinois.

17″ Ring

Finished size	**17″ × 63″**

FABRIC NEEDED (YARDS)	
Background fabric	¾
Print for arcs	1
Posts: two fabrics *each*	¼
Backing and bias binding	2

CUTTING YOUR FABRIC

Use templates S, T, U and V.

Background fabric:

Center: Template S	5
Melon: Template V	16

Print for arcs:

Template T	32

Posts, two fabrics *each*:

Template U	24

1. Join all of the single arcs to the center shapes, as shown in the illustration.

2. Make 16 post units, as shown in the illustration.

3. Join the post units to 3 of the center/arc units to make Unit A. Note the exact placement of the posts, as shown in the illustration.

4. Add melons to the remaining 2 center/arc units to make Unit B, as shown in the illustration.

5. Add color two posts to 4 single arcs to make Unit C's, as shown in the illustration.

6. Add melons to 8 single arcs to make Unit D's, as shown in the illustration.

7. Join all of the units together, referring to the assembly illustration.

8. Attach the remaining post units and color one posts around the edges, as shown in the illustration.

9. Your table runner is ready to be layered and quilted.

10. Finish the edges with a narrow bias binding.

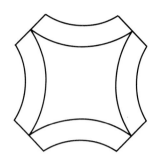

Step 1

Color One *Color Two*

Step 2

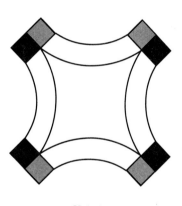

Unit A
Step 3

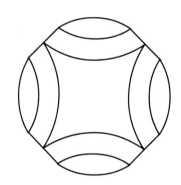

Unit B
Step 4

Color Two *Color Two*

Unit C
Step 5

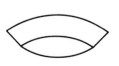

Unit D
Step 6

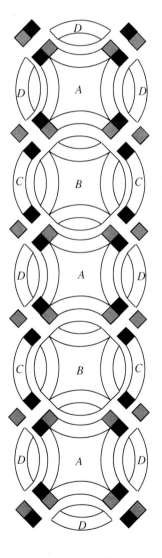

Steps 7-8
Assembly

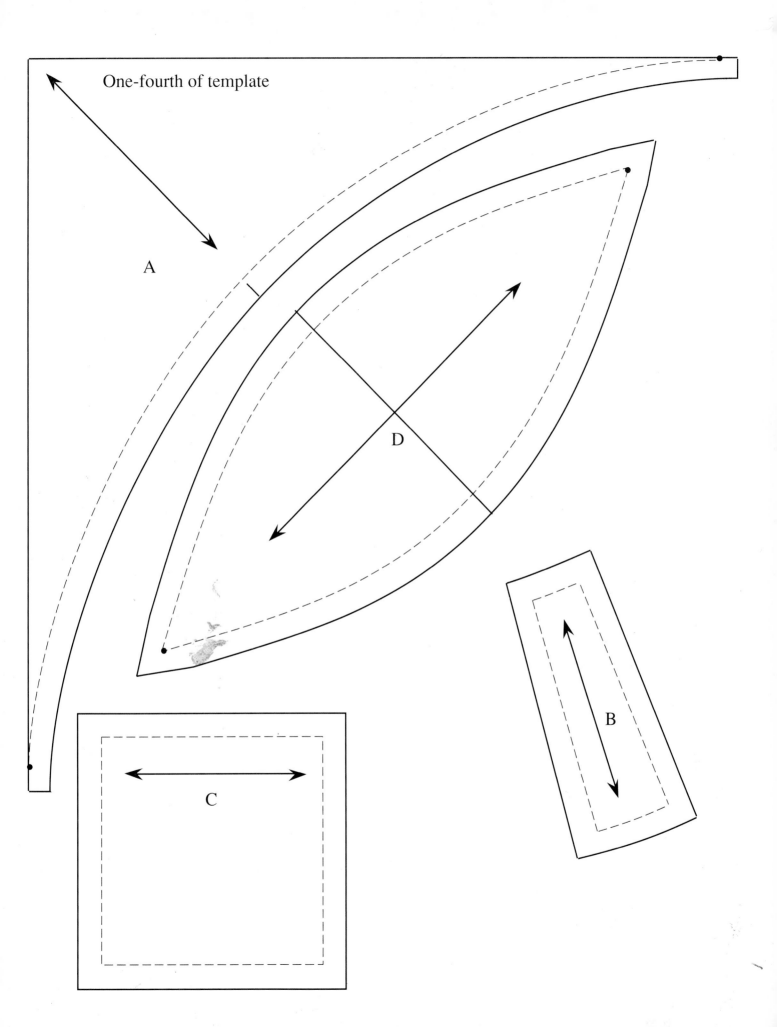

One-fourth of template

A

D

C

B

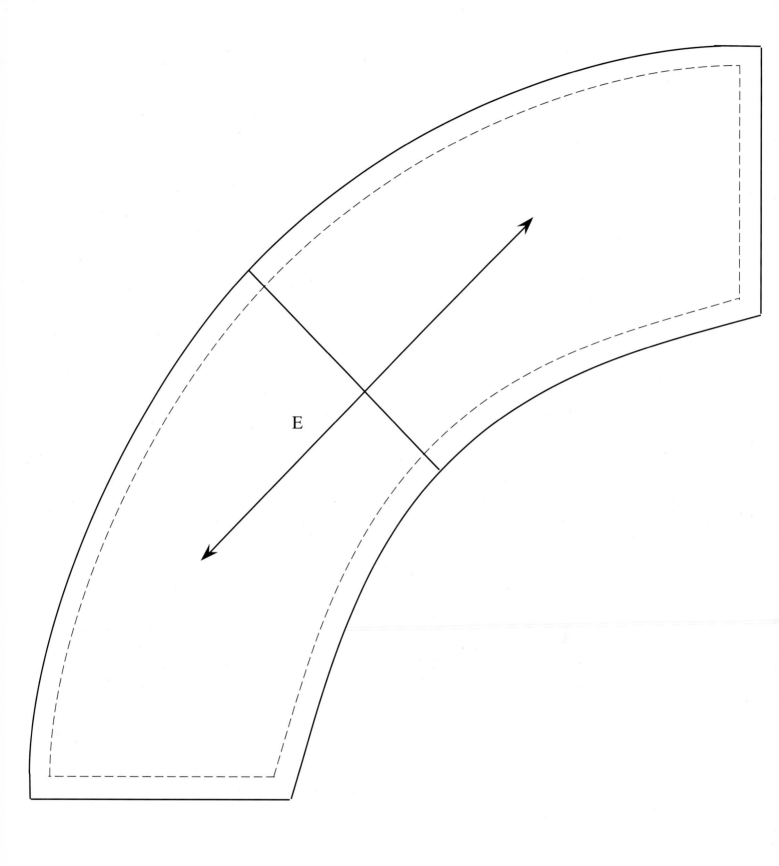

E

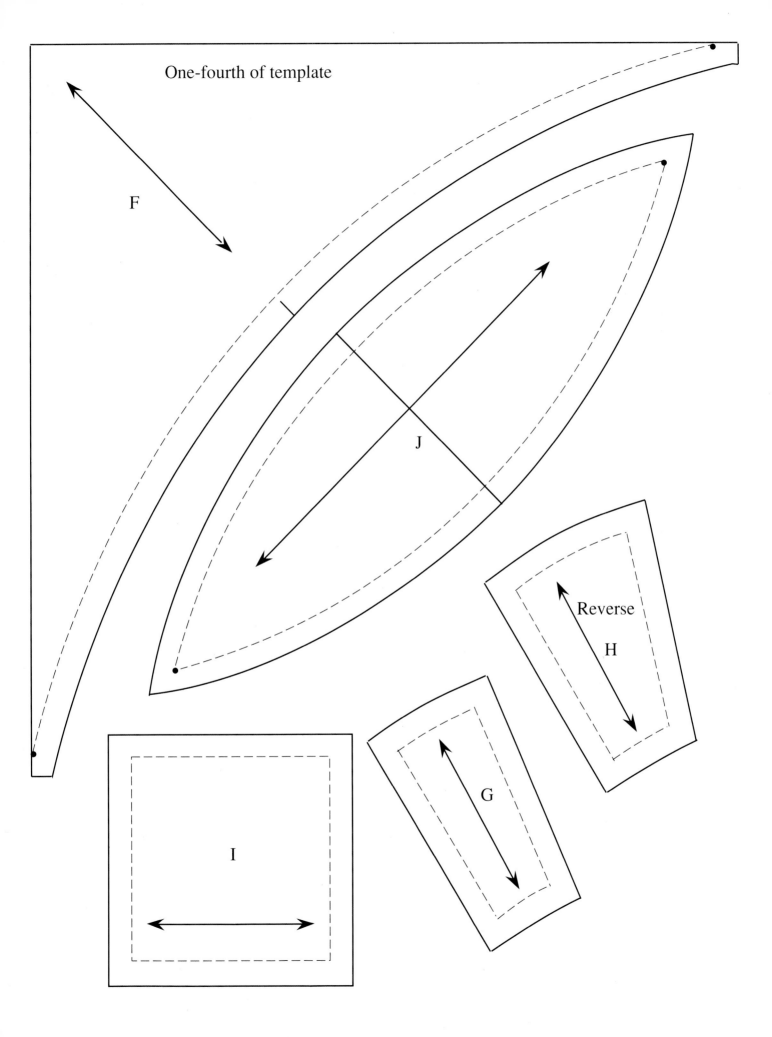

One-fourth of template

F

J

Reverse
H

G

I

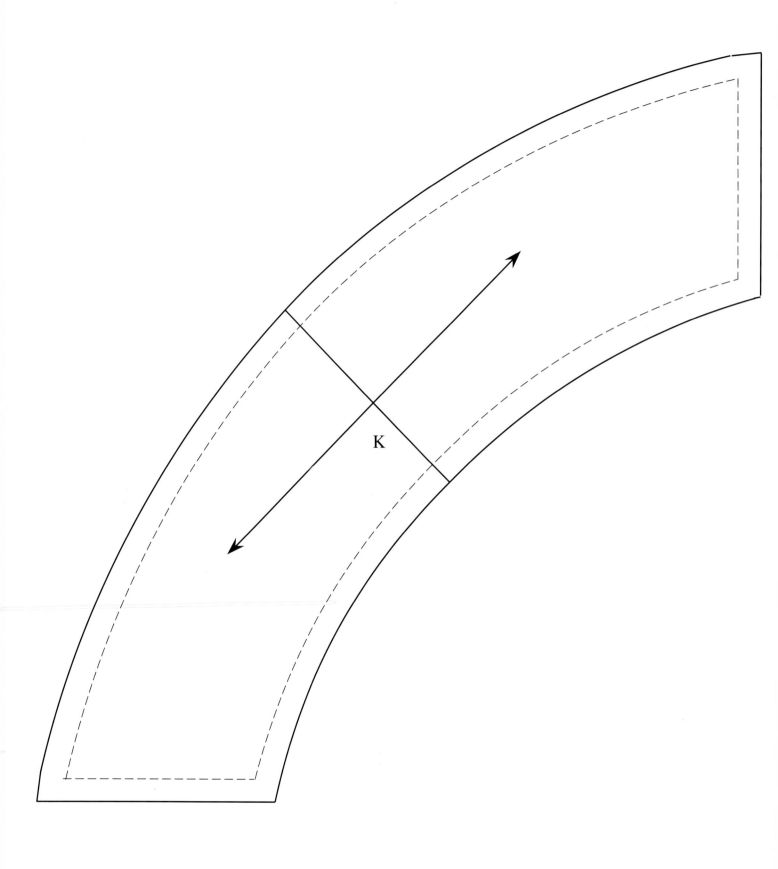

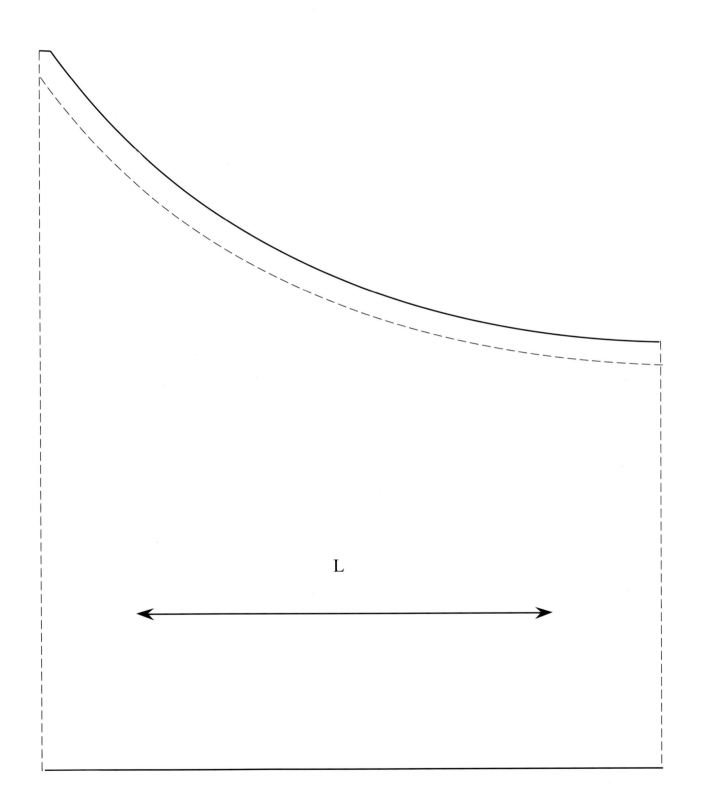

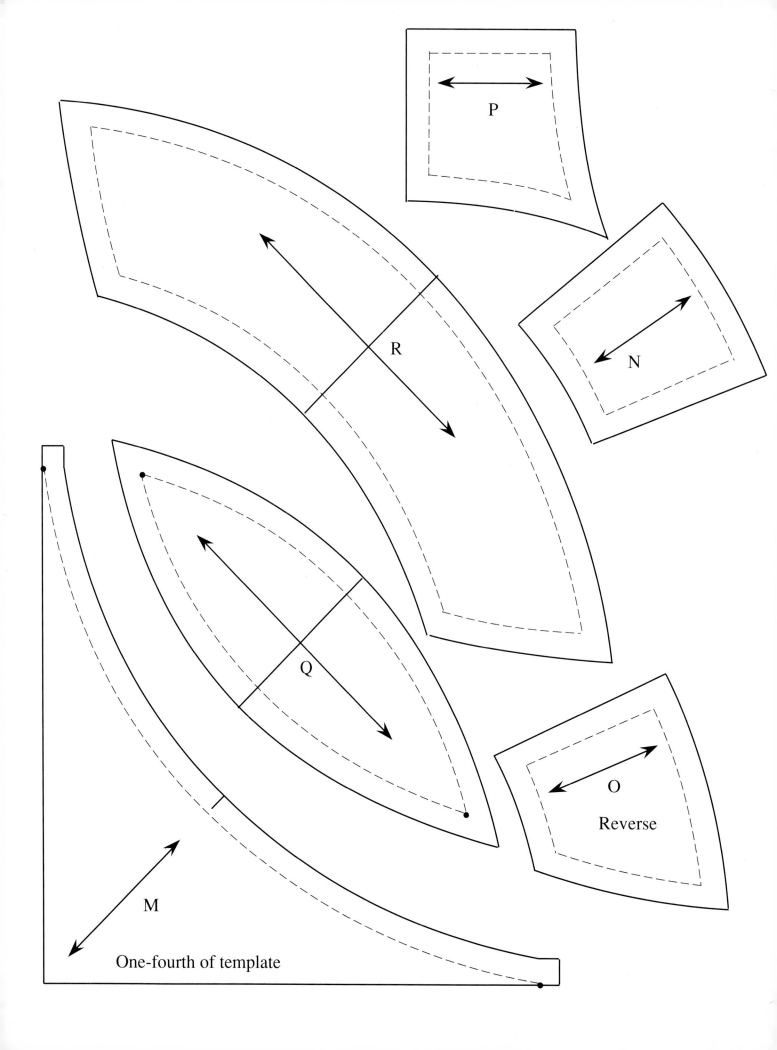

P

N

R

O

Reverse

Q

M

One-fourth of template

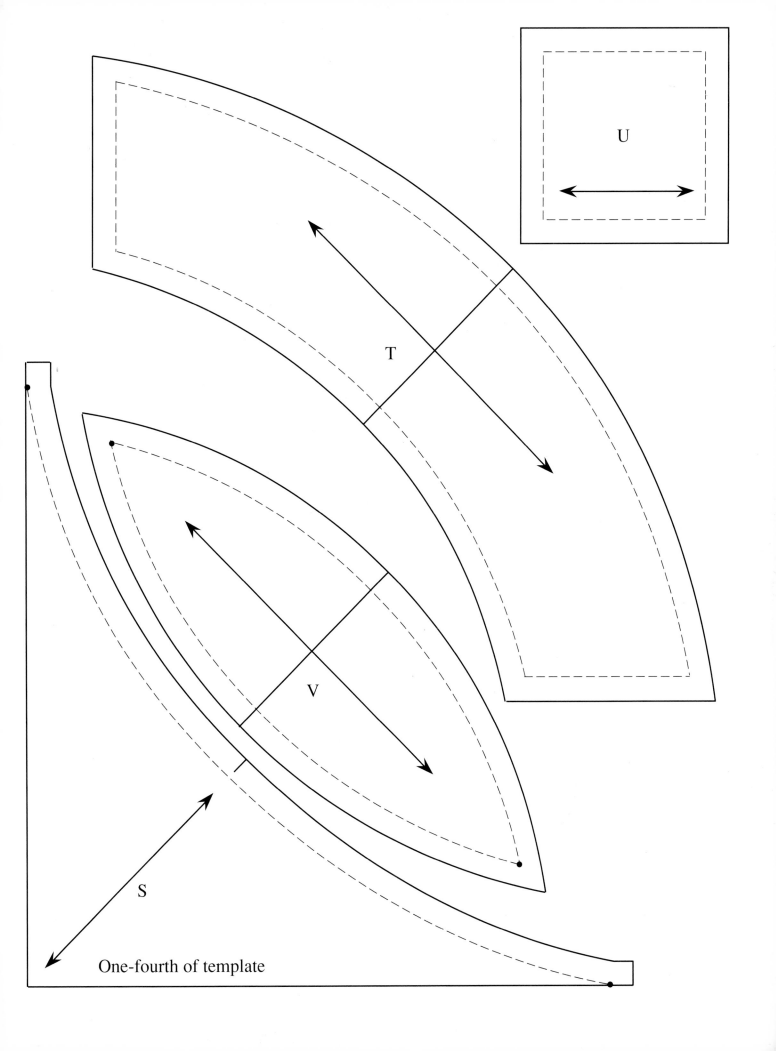

U

T

V

S

One-fourth of template

Simply the Best

THE QUILT DIGEST PRESS

Dept. D
P.O. Box 1331
Gualala, CA 95445